HIDDEN PARTS

Hidden Parts

Mariam Ahmed

Broken Tribe Press

Published by Broken Tribe Press
Lawrence Landing Company
Raleigh, North Carolina 27609
USA, North America

Broken Tribe Press is a proud member of:

Independent Book Publishers Association
    and
Community of Literary Magazines and Presses

Cover art by Jacob Arms

www.brokentribepress.com

BROKEN TRIBE PRESS

Table of Contents

Acknowledgements

FOR AMRAH

Moments of Astral Projection

Asmaan آسمان

A feather in the wind
supreme sky —
my image
A cloud reflects
a mirage
No sound, only breath

Bulbul بلبل

Blowing in warm breeze
under twigs, under wings
Listen...! a flutter

'Bulbul' was me, I
used to whisper
little sounds softly

A nightingale's song / brings me out of a dream / as
the morning glows / This spring is sonorous / and its
song gifted / a thousand notes

I offered my arm
as a new branch

Chamak چمک

Chance brought me here where shadows
Have disappeared under the starry night
And even today the moon is bright
My silhouette reflects
A distance between what is
Known and what is seen

Take away the glimmer / And in its place / Give me /
light / Return to me / my old dreams / As the lines on
my palms / are scarce

So is my time / in this existence / The stars that once /
sat nearby / I cannot see / any longer / Lost in the
ether / They hide / their shine

Duniya دنيا

Days unfold, these worlds crumble
Unwavering breaths swirl --
Now a delicate balance

In the depth of our connection
Your hope cascades into mine
A falling star, a fading breath

> Do you think the stars wish / to touch the earth
> / and hurl themselves / in a burst of fire / not
> dying, exploding / because they cannot / take
> it anymore / not collapsing / pushing /
> through the last piece of power / they have /
> propelling them toward / their dreams —
>
> like me?

Ehsaas احساس

Energies swimming in circles around each
Human's light, bouncing from
Soul to soul

A bright goddess moves through the crowds
A vibration levitating each person with a golden flame
Setting them alight.

> Every living being / radiates this
> energy within / throughout time /
> impacting all that is light / Nothing less
> / Nothing more / just a dimension /
> within the all

Farhat فرحت

From this cliff
Aerial views of the ocean
Radiate salt into my
Hands; the energy
Answers to me
Take all the time you need

Gham غم

Grief consumes the
Hearts of lovers
And
Minds of others

> Let the rain kiss / the top of my head / And let
> it trickle / onto my cheek / Let the pain / sense
> that I / am not dead / and let it / Teach me how
> to / be at ease / Let me feel every / fear of
> dread / and let me find / some kind / of peace

Hamaysha ہمیشہ

How curious that footprints
Are the only mark of
My earthly existence
As they're swept away by
Years of rain
So tell me —
Have you seen any being live beyond its
Age?

Ishq (love) - عشق

Intrinsic desires tell me our
Souls have met before. Destiny wrote our
Hearts together but when I see you why do I
Quiver

Jangal جنگل

Juniper trees under stratus clouds
Azure and lavender across uncut plains
Nettle leaves settled below moving boughs
Grateful blooms sprout through soil
And flowing sunlight peppered by shadows
Long after the air stills

> When I explored
> the muddled woods
> I was lost in
> the tall trees
>
> I was moving
> slowly
> as a stranger
>
> witnessing
> myself clearly
> from above
>
> In search of something
> soft and delicate
> I found
> the river of poetry
>
> with its
> soft, silky flowers
> of gratitude
> blooming there
>
> They were
> transforming
> this wilderness
> into the garden of heaven.

Khwaab خواب

Kempt cloth surrounds me
Holy messages made of my
Waking life
as light
as matter
Believe me

      Little dream, little feeling
      Little talk, little meeting,

      A little in all of life
      Like every time, it happens now

      At some point
      Our caravan stopped,

      Looking for someone
      It remained empty,

      I won these moments
      No dream fulfilled,

      We came to the bend and
      I realize that it's unfinished every time,

      Neither dream nor weave
      A sieve, we live, every feeling
      incomplete

Lamha لمحہ

Like this instance
A last inhale
Millions of stories
Happen in
A span of two moments

Mehsoos محسوس

My fingertips roam
Eternal
Hard rain falling down
Soft metal rooftops

Our memories powerful
Our touches accepting
Speak to me

Naseeb نصيب

Newfound wonders
As yesterday lingers
Seeking hope, soaking in
Every promise
Every laugh, waiting for unexpected
Beginnings

Ojhal اوجهل

Opal wisps pull me from my
Jubilous slumber-verse; as my
Heels touch the ground and my senses
Awaken I am reminded that
Love exists in my dreams

> disappear / like vapor / suspended/ in the air
> / you / on my mind / for an hour / or maybe /
> just a minute / and in the morning / all dull /
> ache / and alone / as I unveil / this new /
> beginning

Pani پانی

Pure rocks in the river
are gently washed by
New hands as they sink
into the sand

Drop / or dribble / a droplet / into / a lake —
wait / for still waters / to see / reflections / of
light / as they slide / across / the water / like
an endless painting / then breathe / again

Qismat قسمت

Quiet storms linger
In these lines
So still, so fortunate
Moons cradle
A prayer
That becomes your lullaby

> Souls of my feet / Dance with ancient bedrock
> / While sweet salty oceans / Run alongside / in
> my blood / Stars of my eyes / See into infinite
> space / Spiraling cellular mysteries /
> Threading through my bones

Roshan روشن

Reflect upon this tinge of pink resting
On the gray evening sky
So content, it falls around me
Humming a familiar song
Among a filtered sun
Now I am free

> Specks, sparkles and reflections / Small
> diamonds, tinsel / and polished platinum /
> Glow in the dark and make / the summer last
> forever / and beyond / Defy the dullness /
> bring home brilliance / Infinity for good
> measure

Sakoon سكون

Stare at the ellipses

At the end of a life story
Keenly they speak of falling
Over the page
Over spaces unknown
New endings, new longings

Tanha تنہا

Then I looked upon
And beyond the
Nacreous daze — a
Haze — and saw that I was
Alone

I think to myself,
"Every voice lives,"

"Which unknown street address is this?"
My eyes ask

> Time is like
> When the falling rain stops
>
> Someone wanders off
> It overshadows our moments,
>
> I think this again, often
> As my watch remains silent

Ugna اگنا

Under the dirt I push my roots
Ground is deeper than I can reach
Night lulls me to sleep and with the sun I
Awaken to spread my leaves

>Brightly illuminated clouds / make us wonder
>– are we in the clouds / looking down on a
>planet / or as we have likely believed / for
>many years / are we on earth / well-grounded
>/ and looking up?

Vakee واقعی

Vivid tales sound
Almost like a fairytale
Keepers of secret whispers
Everything is a game of telephone
Everything is a mirage

> Unseen face / Tight lipped / Secret safe /
> Guarded words / not to give a clue / If you
> knew / what I knew / A secret key / Locked
> away / To keep it hidden / to a dying day

Wakt وقت

Whistle with the winds
At night the stillness sets in
Kindred spirits
Trail my way home

> Silence / on every side / the time likes /
> Making excuses / and stealing / new stories /
> that look old / for many years / Remember /
> every moment's passing / like / cracked
> mirrors / on / broken floors

Xabaan زبان

Xanthic hues of turmeric
Anything for a taste
Bursts of fantasy
A touch of color — just
A dash
Now dive in

Yaad یاد

Your ghost banished
A bit of my heart
And remnants appear when I
Dig deep down

> In my soul / a candle flickers / memory burns
> low / yet still alive / Holding on through /
> bitter frost / a reminder of / how to survive / A
> simple thought / covered by / the snow of time

> What once was lost
> Will again be mine.

Zindagi زندگی

Zoetic words —
I let my voice fill my chest and
Now it cascades out my mouth
Deep down I feel it vibrate
A sublime solitude
Growing
In my mind

Resurrected Infinity

sugar cubes
dangling off rooftops

My dear, it's the
raindrops that sound
like hooves clopping,
earlobe folds focus
audio and hold
onto stampedes
mardis gras beads
and fanciful hand fans
lemon meringue pie

wait in line for
paradise long enough
and purgatory becomes
hellish; dwell on it or
embellish with garlands
of red hot chili peppers

wax, poetic wane
pain neglected stay
in the stream of mind so
copacetic —
steal my sunshine

Resurrected pegasus
starkist, sea shanty
stardust, how far we've come
all unspun so wound up
unfounded but not lost
in this illusion —
full of
psychedelic views &
infinity pools of
possibilities

Spaces Between Spaces

I am
busy killing time

thinking up
singularities, supernovas

fishing for
what is unknown, unseen

I am
fixing my leaking roof

a sorrow I can repair
with pieces of paper

and other scraps
and bits

I am
reading a book

I was in it - about a
dystopia where they

snatch books away
before you have read
them

I am
ending this below

you might consider
it beneath a surface
so much space

between

Ode to Pomegranates

When winter arrives
Delicate seeds fall through my
Crimson-stained fingers

Saturation

where do dreams go
when we awaken?

they dissipate into
unknown dimensions

a portal opens
siphoning

air from my lungs

why is it harder
to breathe

when I'm
with you?

my once
wild thoughts
turning stale quick

after
you spoke
so
soft

leave

my bleeding
  heart
on this tray table

I'm in no upright position

when the oxygen
mask falls
I won't reach for it

the barest glance
upward
        out the window
        it's black
the lights dim

I brace for

this involuntary
voyage into
my soul

it soaks my skin,
  prickles, leaving me
drier than before
I knew you.

touch down: the
  vessel shakes
salty tears
 down my face

landing in
    unknown spaces

time lapses away

water and perfume

sprinkled on soil
will keep her
gravesite cool
and safe

he said, *she's having*
rainbow-flavored
pomegranate seeds
for dessert tonight

an ear to the
headstone,
hands cupped
in supplication

 mom & dad
say, *pray only for*
the best outcome—

     so what
  you wish
cannot cause pain
I'm no stranger
to pain, but
 what's
         on the other side?

when I'm alone
I feel her sometimes
& it reminds me
I have to get up

so I shower, sprinkle
myself with
water and perfume

fix my face

too scared
        to share
 how I
 truly feel—will the
sun disappear?
I'm steady in
this state of mind
 shielded by smoke
from pens & ink that
 cannot run dry
   guarded with
smiles &
   small items—
suddenly, I see
   the future
you're not in it
& I grow sadder
so I smile wider
I love love
 but I don't know
what it is anymore
how to grow it
how to make it
last
longer than
 short
 bursts
what if I became
the rain again?

Ode to Oranges

I love hue,   burst of sun
and citron, life's sweet range —
it's strange how every   segment
resembles a smile
like yours when you sip
from my straw

laughter

I could wrap myself in it

     your laughter

   sleep
     soundly through
cold nights

maybe through
the whole night

I spend
     hours
reading to children
  as they giggle
  at silly rhymes

slipping chocolate into
their hands, delight
in their eyes.

  the sounds, they
    swirl & spiral

   reaching you
in the sky
so I
keep going

Sleep

Ode to Our Cocoon

I love that moment
between space & time — we float
in our own cocoon

Ode to Dreams of You

I saw you in a
dream — my favorite part of
the day is sleep now

Ode to a Shared Pillow

It's the song you play
We lay on the floor sharing
a pillow & warmth

Ode to Silence

& when we sit like
this, side by side in silence
the world feels serene

Ode to Counting

how many ways to
say I love you — I'll count &
tell them all with stars

Keep

Ode to Romantics

it could happen: a
beautiful phrase uttered by
dreaming romantics

Ode to Possibility

opportunity
missed? no — what's meant to be is
not fickle, fleeting

Ode to Your Pen

does your pen move with
thoughts of me flowing down your
heartfelt fingertips?

Ode to Lips

my lips have over
a million nerve endings &
you're on every one

Ode to Feathers
I share with you: songs
& books, touches & soft looks —
feathers flown away

Pull of Sleep

A   vine
expands   its   grasp
over neglected backyards

Broken   fence
 staggering
slow   fall

The lighting starts
young   with   wildness
Pearl white
as the gardenias   see fit

They   seem to linger   in the   mist
   waiting

Then   as   the   sun   sets
the   sky   hushes   through
dirty mauve   to   dull blue
The   color perhaps
of a   still   sea.

Even now in winter
Even now somewhere

Peony   sky
And   I
am within the   wide   wide
   Opening,

It could have hollowed out a flower in me

We are also created
For anything good
No, not just imagination
I know this.

Uninstall

Unimpressive places line sidewalks
Uncorking thoughts outside my head

Uncanny clown faces
Crowd unimportant stations

Uninterrupted I remain
Under oceans, skies, and stars

Unladylike, they call me
Undaunted, I walk away

Unreal, this underworld
Untroubled, I uninstall

Tip my hat unintentionally
Encore for the underdog.

Ode to a Coffee Stain

Forming a heart shape
Stain on the carpet
Coffee has feelings

current sea

I was born atop the back of something
silver

was it waves and waters; a tipped
chalice, old worlds
poured away —

or fleeting
mist, too old to stay?

Orion's Halo

a crown   circles

around   saturn

soft   static

scattered   sonic

rings   she

sings:

I can   see your

halo   halo

halo

It's the halo effect

it kicks in &
we're off like a rocket
can't stop it

anything wrong
we get off it, no problem

closer to god
with this face

it works
nine times
out of ten
at least

nice chain, they admire

looking on with desire
while I catch
        classic cars
in my mitt
            amidst wealth
                        I acquire

  all around us, hollers
Gold, Oil, & Dollars
each line by design
        my candy paint
in your pallet
I sell it
    with relish & embellish
I've had it —

        she said,
"the world around you
        is off, I can feel it,"

she sees what she wants
        to see, he hears what he wants
        to hear, a sphere, a marble
quick darts in my heart —

  can't fake anything
        you'd sense it
  with questions
& find out what
happened, I imagine

            a new world can

    last   when

      our luck   switches

                patterns

Cirrus

gray streak
a single stroke
splayed on canvas
I thought about it
all day

Held up two fingers
with lavender polish
Le bonheur sur lèvres,
un peu naïvement

She smirked
with dulcet scorn,
turned a corner

Some days
looking up
to the
Cerulæn sky
is everything

gravity

I was unsure the moon knew of me
I shouted up
Sent a letter via pigeon mail
Spoke to the stars to put a good word in for me
I got nothing back
Then I realized
the moon shines to show
a way through the dark
brightening;
the best response

Some Constellation

beside the granite door
a sheen of dust disturbed
by fingers
chairs lined in a row
curved in a crescent
around the casket
sun dips into water and
we can see the graves
outside the window
crystal sand and stones
mapping out
some constellation

Poem of Tomorrow

We float high out in space,
whistling among stars
 cars art shopping cart k-mart
rainbows chrome hearts blue sun
shine and sweet tarts raining from
above the world.
precious pieces of nature
lifting spirit away.
 shelves filled: blue
and green cactus flowers grass dew
wooden twigs; such soot
sprites scatter when moments fade
into stellar distance
We believe in tomorrow

Mow a Maze

azure   fields
  candlelit   mazes
 drop   in,
   wander,
follow
    cadence
    turn
left   at a
   skull-shaped
          stone,
zig-zag   down
   an   alleyway —
what if   I stayed?
   took a   breather.
I tried to find her,
   I tried to leave her
lightly   stepping,
  hiding,
  wedged between
two   hedges —
crimson   leaves
  cut   through
my   skin

I pray for   ease
&   mention,
  "I   can't   take
it   anymore"
 my   throat —
    it's   sore

from   speaking
    I know I
talk   too much.

    craving
  invisible
stay   quiet
  stay   still
stay   still!
   stay   quiet!
stay   quiet
  silent
I cannot
  see   you
I cannot
   be   you
The time is now
  break   some   branches
mow   the   maze
  light   a   few   matches
set   it
  on   fire
this   sleepy
  desire
when   I
  awaken
I'll   forget
  you.
I'll   forget   you.
  don't   forget
I'll
   forget   you.

Enjoy   my
  maze, I'm
gone   already

 burned
  it away
walking on
  ashes

unsteady
  these   lazy
mazes: I've
  lit   up
  so   many

November

I was transfixed, my tears falling freely
I touched the hospital gown lightly
and placed butterfly wings on
her fingers, she flew away gently

A smile shaped her lips later
Inside, I was torn asunder
Fall has arrived and I miss her
Blue and white roses this November

You Belong Here

At a sticky café table in Karachi,
my father's voice mingled with the city's:
Picture a fountain —
pigeons pecking, gray
against the bright plume of peacocks,
two worlds never touching.
But one pigeon, captivated by colors,
dreamed of joining their dance.
The others laughed,
called it foolish,
but the pigeon gathered
fallen peacock feathers,
pinned them to its plain wings,
and with this patchwork of pride
approached the bright flock.
The peacocks saw through the disguise,
the false feathers falling,
and cast the pigeon out,
their contempt sharp as their tails.
Rejected, it turned back to its own —
only to find it too was a stranger there,
mocked for its longing, for daring to change.
Alone, it wandered,
belonging to neither sky nor ground.
In the heat, I wondered —
Why did the pigeon stay,
and not fly far away?

Am I the pigeon, or the peacock,
or some other bird entirely,
lost in the branches of this tangled belonging?

Acknowledgments

Poems in this book first appeared in various forms in the following publications:

The Offending Adam: "Moments of Astral Projection"
Progenitor Art and Literary Journal:
 "Resurrected Infinity"
The Elevation Review: "Spaces Between Spaces"
Midway Journal: "Ode to Pomegranates"
Ignatian Literary Magazine: "Saturation"
Kitchen Table Quarterly: "Ode to Oranges"
Flint Hills Review: "Laughter"
Panorama: The Journal of Travel, Place, and Nature:
"Sleep/Keep"
Cradle of Balladry: "Pull of Sleep
Maintenant 13: "Uninstall"
Press Pause Press: "current sea"
Al Dente: "Ode to a Coffee Stain"
Dipity Literary Magazine: "November"
Moonlighting by Lit Pub: "You Belong Here"

ABOUT THE AUTHOR

Mariam Ahmed is a Californian poet.